They Also
Serve...

THEY ALSO SERVE...
Tennis – A Global Religion

Written by Ralph Wright, OSB
Illustrations by Ralph Wright, OSB

Library of Congress Cataloguing-in-Publication Data

Wright, Ralph OSB
They Also Serve . . . Tennis–A Global Religion

Design & Cover Art by William Mathis, MathisJones Communications, LLC

Published by Monograph Publishing, LLC
1 Putt Lane
Eureka, Missouri 63025

ISBN# 978-0-9799482-8-2

11 9 8 7 6 5 4 3 2

Signature Book Printing, Inc
www.sbpbooks.com
First printing, May 2011
Printed in the U.S.A.

DEDICATION

To the happy memory
of
Albert J. Bedard, Jr.
March 20, 1926 – July 18, 2010
who
whether he was
serving
hamburgers, fish, banana bread
or gasoline
did it always
with his friends & customers in mind.

THEY ALSO SERVE . . .
CONTENTS

Global Religion

brings humor smack back into the center of sport. The sport 'pie,' that goes back way beyond Homer, has many ingredients. Fun, recreation, competition, exercise, teamwork, entertainment — all play various roles in various games. Recently work, money and politics have taken some sports by storm. In *They Also Serve...Tennis — A Global Religion*, the 'good laugh and quiet smile' of *Wild...* takes a step further. By bringing "clerical" figures — Cardinals, Popes, Imams, Rabbis and Abbesses — onto the tennis court, their "decorum" is shattered and a low key chuckle emerges. Humor and tennis are both cohesive — they bring people together as in the original Olympics for peaceful, enjoyable, channelled competition. Winning no longer entails annihilating the opponent but relishing the challenge, fostering prowess, dexterity and achievement. Perhaps sportsmanship can trickle down into world religion.

Ralph Wright, OSB

THEY ALSO SERVE...

Tennis – A Global Religion

Written by Ralph Wright, OSB
Illustrations by Ralph Wright, OSB

A cardinal from Alabama
has a serve with a Wimbledon glamour.
His amazing ace
has incredible pace
and blitzes the line like a hammer.

A nun on a trip to Bermuda
was chased by a vast barracuda,
'till with blunt metal racket
she turned to attack it
and killed it before it had chewed her.

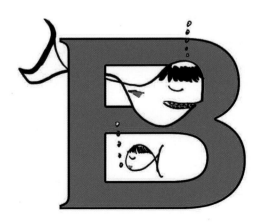

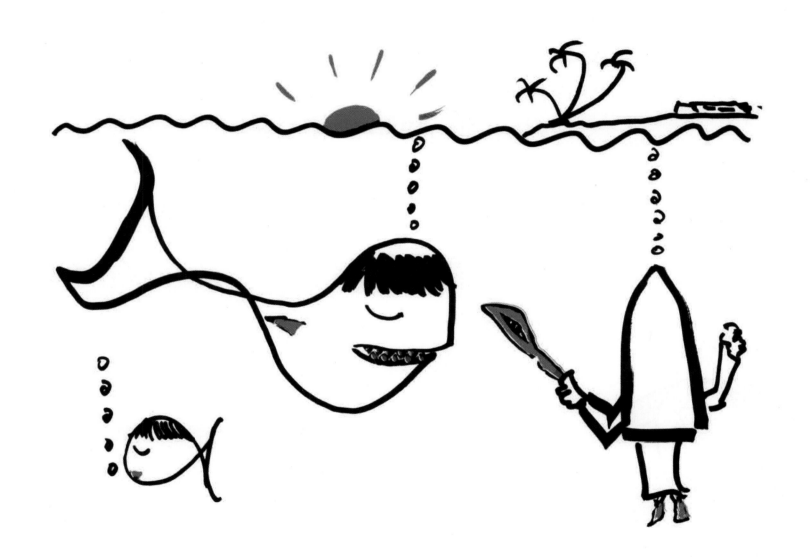

A compassionate abbess from Crete
finds it desperately hard to compete.
When she's winning a game
she feels so much shame
that she prays for the grace of defeat.

A monk who serves fast in Duluth
spins twisters and curvers to boot.
But his lack of control
keeps him deep in the hole
and his comments are often uncouth.

A friar born in Elkhorn, Nebraska
has a game-plan as cool as Alaska —
he consistently waits
'till it's almost too late
then hacks his way back from disaster.

A drop-shooting sister from France,
whose feet tread a lyrical dance,
should give some reflection
to more genuflection
for grace should leave nothing to chance.

A steam-hammer nun from Geneva,
a heavy-weight over-achiever,
would smite with the crash
of her overhead smash
her victim — then trample and leave her.

A guru who combs Honolulu,
has a grip that's as rigid as glue-lu.
His backswing is smooth
as fingers that soothe
but, alas, he has no follow-thru-lu.

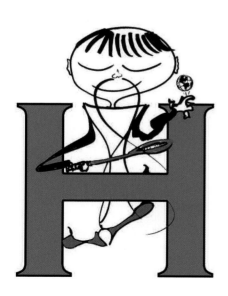

A smooth young recluse from Iran,
who oozes a cadillac charm,
is perfecting his aces
in private oases
with rackets entirely of palm.

A young buddhist monk from Japan,
who ponders the essence of Man,
with noble reserve
can return any serve
and knows with calm that he can.

A monk, who plays sheikhs in Kuwait,
can land any lob on a plate.
He hits it high over
the sheikh's left shoulder,
who turns and trots back - but too late!

When a highly strung bishop from Leeds,
whose ulcer still pains him and bleeds,
diverts his high tensions
to catgut dimensions
his thoughts are as calm as his deeds.

A hermit, who prays near Manila,
used to hit with a lady guerrilla,
'till his temper got frayed
and he served a grenade
in a futile endeavor to kill her.

A primitive nun from Nevada
plays net for her cannibal father.
When she misses a sitter
he threatens to hit her
and leave her for stew in his larder.

An imam, who taught in Oman
and bows down to Mecca at dawn,
claims that all his aggressions
through tennis are lessened
— which helps him to live the Koran.

A young liturgist from Peru,
thinks the rubrics for hitting are few:
hit it *in* and with spice,
let it *never* bounce twice,
hit it *over* the net and not through.

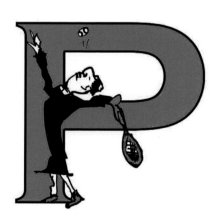

A rabbi, who played near Qumran,
had a voice with a lyrical charm.
He would serve with a roll
of Dead Sea scroll
and mellow each ace with a psalm.

The ghost of a hermit from Rome
had a ball made entirely of stone.
When haunting he'd slam it
at back walls of granite —
for always he haunted alone.

A hilarious nun from Seville,
whose talent was practically nil,
found tennis such fun
that she usually won
— her laughter she used with great skill.

An abbot, who serves in Tibet,
hits volleys that no one can get.
His overhead's calmer
than many a lama
and no one can pass him at net.

A patriarch from the Ukraine,
whose tennis is largely in vain,
swings wide at the ball,
never hits it at all —
and everyone else is to blame.

The cardinal bishop of Venice
excels at pontifical tennis.
With crozier racket
he can sometimes hack it
but his mitre is rather a menace.

A witch with a cauldron in Wales
brews magic with vipers and snails.
Though the taste of her brew
claims a victim or two
her aces come when she inhales.

Pope Kubla from Xanadu-Rome
built a Vatican Sports Pleasuredome.
Whence he served to far places
encyclical aces
on balls branded Ex-Cathedrome.

An abbess from fair Yokohama
plays tennis with God without drama.
Though he serves from above
and it's Forty, Love,
yet nothing he does can alarm her.

An exorcist from the Zambesi
thinks tennis is really damned easy.
But the gleam in his eye
as he pounds the ball by
makes even the demons uneasy.

THWACK

walking between
the dark green
heavy plastic
end curtains
and the stark wall
in the indoor tennis club last night
as the heavy popping thud of racket
striking ball
hit my ears
I suddenly wondered
why
the relatively sane men
and saner women
from Homer's day
down to our own
have whiled away with such relish
endless hours
thwacking or watching others thwack
a bland ball

unless it's because we're genetically bound
to mirror our Father
whose glorious mischievous
somehow superfluous
always mysterious
cosmic game
we now eternally are

BETWEEN SERVES

As each point ends
and I win or lose
a positive stance
is what I choose.

If an unforced error
has spelt defeat,
in my lap-top mind
I hit delete.

Relaxed, unrushed,
I move to the line.
My body obeys
my confident mind.

I plan the path
of my coming serve.
Then the ritual starts
that nothing disturbs.

BULLET SERVE

With a ritual bounce
I create my calm,
then reach up high
with the tossing arm.

The ball soars smooth
to beyond my reach.
My eyes stay glued
to the fur of the peach.

My knees coil bent
like a spring for power,
and all lash through
at contact hour.

I nail that ball
as my arm pronates,
and I follow through
for a sizzling ace.

Ralph Wright OSB
2011

THE END

They Also Serve...